How To Give A Great Presentation

Presentation techniques that will transform a speech into a memorable event

"Practical, proven techniques that will help you to make your next speech a success"

Dr. Jim Anderson

Published by:
Blue Elephant Consulting
Tampa, Florida

Copyright © 2013 by Dr. Jim Anderson

All rights reserved. No part of this book may be reproduced of transmitted in any form or by any means, electronic or mechanical, including photocopying, recording or by any information storage and retrieval system without written permission of the publisher, except for inclusion of brief quotations in a review.

Printed in the United States of America

Library of Congress Control Number: 2013957206

ISBN-13: 978-1494419097
ISBN-10: 1494419092

Warning – Disclaimer

The purpose of this book is to educate and entertain. This book does not promise or guarantee that anyone following the ideas, tips, suggestions, techniques or strategies will be hired. It is the discretion of employers if you will or will not be hired. The author, publisher and distributor(s) shall have neither liability nor responsibility to anyone with respect to any loss or damage caused, or alleged to be caused, directly or indirectly by the information contained in this book.

Recent Books By The Author

Product Management

- Product Development Lessons For Product Managers: How Product Managers Can Create Successful Products

- Customer Lessons For Product Managers: Techniques For Product Managers To Better Understand What Their Customers Really Want

Public Speaking

- How To Rehearse In Order To Give The Perfect Speech: How to effectively rehearse your next speech to that your message be remembered forever!

- Secrets To Creating The Perfect Speech: How to create a speech that will make your message be remembered forever!

CIO Skills

- How CIOs Can Make Innovation Happen: Tips And Techniques For CIOs To Use In Order To Make Innovation Happen In Their IT Department

- CIO Communication Skills Secrets: Tips And Techniques For CIOs To Use In Order To Become Better Communicators

IT Manager Skills

- Secrets Of Effective Leadership For IT Managers: Tips And Techniques That IT Managers Can Use In Order To Develop Leadership Skills

- IT Manager Career Secrets: Tips And Techniques That IT Managers Can Use In Order To Have A Successful Career

Negotiating

- Learn How To Argue In Your Next Negotiation: How To Develop The Skill Of Effective Arguing In A Negotiation In Order To Get The Best Possible Outcome

- How To Open Your Next Negotiation: How To Start A Negotiation In Order To Get The Best Possible Outcome

Miscellaneous

- Power Distribution Unit (PDU) Secrets: What Everyone Who Works In A Data Center Needs To Know!

- Making The Jump: How To Land Your Dream Job When You Get Out Of College!

Note: See a complete list of books by Dr. Jim Anderson at the back of this book.

Acknowledgements

Any book like this one is the result of years of real-world work experience. In my over 25 years of working for 7 different firms, I have met countless fantastic people and I've been mentored by some truly exceptional ones. Although I've probably forgotten some of the people who made me the person that I am today, here is my attempt to finally give them the recognition that they so truly deserve:

- Thomas P. Anderson
- Art Puett
- Bobbi Marshall
- Bob Boggs

Dr. Jim Anderson

This book is dedicated to my wife Lori. None of this would have been possible without her love and support.

Thanks for the best 21 years of my life (so far)...!

Table Of Contents

HOW TO GIVE A GREAT PRESENTATION 8

ABOUT THE AUTHOR 10

CHAPTER 1: CONSTRUCTIVE CRITICISM: "HOW CAN I SAY THIS NICELY?" 15

CHAPTER 2: DO CEO'S COMMUNICATE BETTER THAN COMMON FOLK? 18

CHAPTER 3: I WANT TO PRESENT JUST LIKE STEVE JOBS DID 21

CHAPTER 4: I HEAR YOUR BODY TALKING… 24

CHAPTER 5: 5 WAYS TO DELIVER A DISASTROUS PRESENTATION 27

CHAPTER 6: TOP 9 BAD HABITS OF TECHNICAL PRESENTERS 31

CHAPTER 7: PUBLIC SPEAKING PROBLEM: TOO MANY QUESTIONS (FROM ONE PERSON)! 35

CHAPTER 8: STAND UP STRAIGHT YOUNG MAN! (PUBLIC SPEAKING TIP) 39

CHAPTER 9: WELCOME TO THE POD: TIPS ON PODCASTING FOR PUBLIC SPEAKERS 42

CHAPTER 10: 4 THINGS A PUBLIC SPEAKER NEEDS TO KNOW ABOUT WEBCONFERENCING 46

CHAPTER 11: PRESENTATION FROM A BOOK: HOW TO DO DRAMATIC READINGS 49

CHAPTER 12: 10 TIPS FOR LITTLE PRESENTATIONS (OR PRESENTATIONS TO LITTLE PEOPLE) 54

How To Give A Great Presentation

After the speech has been written, the practice has been done, all that is left is for you to actually present your speech to the audience. It goes without saying that this can be one of life's biggest challenges!

It turns out that it really should not be. Assuming that you've been able to collect your thoughts, write them down, and have had the time to practice what you want to say, then everything should go ok.

However, I suspect that you'd like to do better than "ok". As long as you are taking the time to create and practice a speech, you sure want the speech to make an impact on your audience. You want to be able to deliver a great speech.

It turns out that you can do this, you just need to know how to go about doing it. That's exactly what this book is going to do. I'm going to show you what you need to know in order to make sure that your next speech is one that your audience will remember long after you are done speaking.

In order to make this happen we're going to have to talk about how Steve Jobs used to give speeches. We're going to have to talk about your body language and what it may be telling your audience.

It turns out that your posture is also important and so we should talk about that. Finally, not every speech is the same. We'll talk about how you can get ready for speeches that you give in unique situations.

In the end, you'll have a very good insight into how you can make your next presentation the best that you've ever given. Ultimately the impact of your speech will be determined by the quality of your presentation.

For more information on what it takes to be a great public speaker, check out my blog, The Accidental Communicator, at:

www.TheAccidentalCommunicator.com

Good luck!

- Dr. Jim Anderson

About The Author

I must confess that I never set out to be a public speaker. When I went to school, I studied Computer Science and thought that I'd get a nice job programming and that would be that. Well, at least part of that plan worked out!

My first job was working for Boeing on their F/A-18 fighter jet program. I spent my days programming fighter jet software in assembly language and I loved it. The U.S. government decided to save some money and went looking for other countries to sell this plane to. This put me into an unfamiliar role: I started to meet with foreign military officials and I ended up having to give speeches in order to explain what my product did.

Time moved on and so did I. I found myself working for Siemens, the big German telecommunications company. They were making phone switches and selling them to the seven U.S. phone companies. The problem was that the switches were too complicated. Customers couldn't tell the difference between one complicated phone switch from another complicated phone switch. Once again I found myself standing in front of the room giving speeches in order to explain what these complicated machines did and why ours were better than anyone else's.

I've spent over 25 years working as a product manager for both big companies and startups. This has given me an opportunity to do many, many presentations for customers, at conferences, and everywhere in-between.

I now live in Tampa Florida where I spend my time managing my consulting business, Blue Elephant Consulting, teaching college courses at the University of South Florida, and traveling to work with companies like yours to share the knowledge that I have about how to create and deliver powerful and effective speeches.

I'm always available to answer questions and I can be reached at:

Dr. Jim Anderson
Blue Elephant Consulting
Email: jim@BlueElephantConsulting.com
Facebook: http://goo.gl/1TVoK
Web: **www.BlueElephantConsulting.com**

"Unforgettable communication skills that will set your ideas free…"

Create Speeches That Motivate Your Audiences And Get Your Message Heard!

Dr. Jim Anderson is available to provide training and coaching on the topics that are the most important to people who have to speak in public: how can I create a speech that people want to hear and how can I deliver in a way that will allow me to connect with my audience and get my point across to them?

Dr. Anderson believes that in order to both learn and remember what he says, speakers need to laugh. Each one of his speeches is full of fun and humor so that what he says "sticks" with everyone.

Dr. Anderson's Public Speaking Training Includes:

1. How to plan your next speech: pick your purpose and understand your audience.
2. What's the best way to get PowerPoint and Keynote to work with you, not against you?
3. What do you need to do when you are presenting in order to truly connect with your audience?

Dr. Jim Anderson presents over 100 speeches per year. To invite Dr. Anderson to speak at your event, contact him at:

Phone: 813-418-6970 or
Email: jim@BlueElephantConsulting.com

Blue Elephant Consulting

Speaking   Negotiating   Managing   Marketing

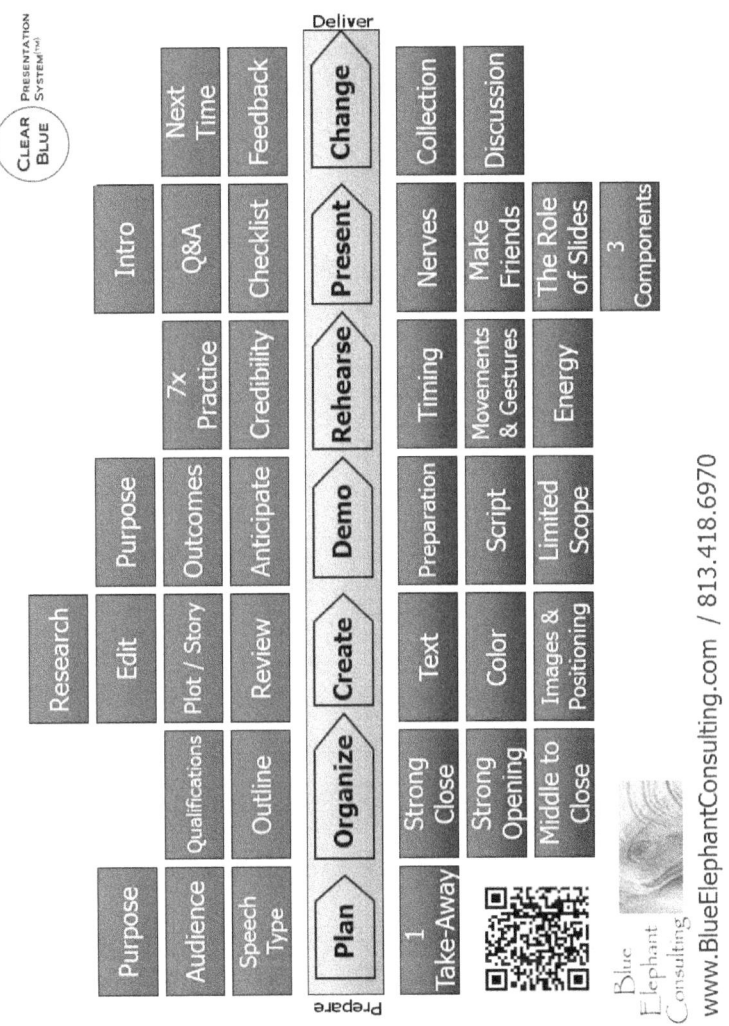

Blue Elephant Consulting has created the **Clear Blue™ Presentation System** for creating and delivering powerful and memorable presentations. The contents of this book are based on lessons learned during the development of the Clear Blue system. Contact Blue Elephant Consulting to learn more about the Clear Blue presentation system.

Chapter 1

Constructive Criticism: "How Can I Say This Nicely?"

Chapter 1: Constructive Criticism: "How Can I Say This Nicely?"

Last week I was invited to sit in on two sets of presentations by junior members of a very large telecommunication firm's IT department. They are part of a management training program and the program's instructors asked me to visit because they had had some guest presenters who were *really* bad.

The hope was that I could provide immediate feedback for the teams that presented as well as things to avoid for the teams that had yet to present. Sounded fair enough, eh?

During the presentations I wrote notes like a madman. Ten separate engineers presented material and I filled about seven pages of a notebook with comments and ideas. To keep things brief, let me share with you the top three things that I noticed:

1. **Who You Talking To?**: Each and every one of the presenters spent a lot of their "stage time" with their bodies pointed towards the projection screen and actually talked to the screen instead of the audience. This happens way too often when you use PowerPoint to create an outline of you speech and end up reading it off of the screen.

Solution: The correct way to present material is to make sure that you always face your audience. The slides are there to reinforce your verbal message — you should spend no time staring at them. Instead, have a conversation with your audience and let us choose if we want to look at you or your slide.

2. **Here? There? Over There?**: Just where to stand was a major problem for each presenter. There was a lectern on the stage and nobody seemed to know what to do with it (def: a lectern is

big and goes all the way down to the floor, a podium is shorter and generally sits on a table. They are both used to hold a speaker's notes.) Some stood behind it, some stood off to its side, and some completely ignored it. They all moved from behind it to in front of it and back during their presentations. The end result was that this turned out to be a distraction to everyone who was watching the presentations.

Solution:: Make a decision before you start to speak — in front of the lectern or behind it. Once you make this decision, stick with it. Neither decision is right or wrong, only alternating between the two positions is wrong because it becomes distracting.

3. **Handy Hands:** Hands sure are nice to have. Except when you are presenting to a group. Then the difficult question of what to do with your hands when you aren't making a gesture comes up.

Each of the 10 engineers who presented did something different with their hands: in the pockets, behind the back, crossed in front, praying that they don't get kicked in the groin, etc. What this ended up doing was to once again distract the audience as we watched the speaker try to determine with what to do with their hands.

Solution: When not using them as a part of your speech, let your hands drop to your sides and let them dangle there. This sounds soooo easy; however, it really is quite difficult to do. If you spend time practicing talking in front of a mirror at home, you'll be able to catch yourself doing "handy" things and can quickly put a stop to it.

Chapter 2

Do IT CEO's Communicate Better Than Common Folk?

Chapter 2: Do CEO's Communicate Better Than Common Folk?

I had an opportunity to attend the very large trade show that was put on by the giant storage company EMC. It was held in Las Vegas and I only lost about $100 or so gambling!

The thing that I liked best about attending this show was that if I moved quickly, I could get a front row seat for the keynote addresses that were given by EMC's upper level management team. I was only vaguely interested in what they had to say, but I was VERY interested in how they would say it and if any of it would stick.

During the big kickoff Joe Tucci who is the Chairman, President, and CEO of this $15B firm talked. I had very high hopes: I mean, if anyone could buy their way to being an effective technical communicator, then Joe is the man.

So how did he do? Sadly, I believe that I'd have to give him a C. Maybe a C+, but that's it. He did a fantastic job of delivering a speech from a technical point of view: clear diction, no filler words, very little pacing, and his slides / graphics were top notch (but of course — he's in charge of a $15B company!).

So why does he just get a grade of C? He didn't connect with his audience. He talked for about an hour and must have hit on about 40 different points during his talk about EMC the company and all of its products and upcoming products.

However, I'm betting that 30 minutes after he was done, you could pull aside anyone who had attended and they'd be unable to remember more than one or two things that Joe said. When it was over, it was over — the world had not been changed. What a waste!

I need to give Joe one little out here: he is in charge of the company. What he says can cause a change in the company's stock price and so he always has to be careful about what he says. However, that doesn't mean that he can get away with being boring.

Complaining is easy. Now how about if we talk about what Joe could have done differently to have been a more effective communicator.

#1: know your audience, tailor your communication to your audience. Joe's audience was VERY technical. These are the people who live, eat, breath storage systems for a living. Joe talked at a very high level for his whole speech and thus didn't connect with anyone in the audience. He needed to at least once drop down into their world, show that he knows the types of challenges that they are facing, and then move on.

#2: Where's the passion? Joe delivered his entire speech in a flat, non-emotional tone. Yawn! Come on, Joe's from Boston the home of notorious hot heads. Oh, and he's a sales guy to his core. Get some of that passion to come out — get people fired up! Tell the audience that HP and IBM make lousy products and that they made the right decision by selecting EMC products. Whatever — just show that you really care about this stuff.

#3: Tell a story. Nowhere in Joe's speech did he include a story. Stories are how we have always learned. If Joe had included a story, then this is what everyone would have remembered long after he was done.

So to answer the original question: no, CEO's don't necessarily do a better job of communicating than you or I do. Good communication always comes down to the three basics: know your audience, care about what you are taking about, and use stories to give your audience a way to remember what you have said.

Chapter 3

I Want To Present Just Like Steve Jobs Did

Chapter 3: I Want To Present Just Like Steve Jobs Did

Well, at least I sure would like to be able to give a speech like he did. Every time Steve gave a speech, he did a great job of giving the Apple corporate pitch. Clearly he had a nature skill for giving a great speech. We may never be as good at public speaking as Steve was; however, we sure can learn from him. Here are five quick tips from Steve to you:

1. **Benefits NOT Features**: This is where Steve was at his best. In his speeches he spent his time talking about the experience of using the product, not how the product was implemented. Instead of talking about the 30GB memory size of an iPod, instead he'd talk about the 7,500 songs that it can carry, or the 25,000 photos that it can carry, or the 75 hours of video that it can carry.

2. **Practice and Then Practice Some More**: Steve was the CEO of Apple and a board member of Disney. You'd think that he'd have a team of speech writers create his speeches and then he'd just grab it, scan it, and jump up on the stage and give it. Nope, it turns out that he spent hours upon hours practicing each speech. A 2006 Business Week article reported that Steve would spend at least four hours going over every slide and every part of a demonstration as he prepared for a presentation.

3. **A Picture Is Worth…**: Have you ever seen a picture or a video from one of Steve's presentations? There are either no words or very few words on the slides that were displayed on the giant screens behind him. There are certainly no lists of bullet points. Steve (and his highly paid set of presentation artists) understood that it's really his words that counted — the slides were just

there to support his message.

4. **Energy + Enthusiasm = Passion**: Every time Steve spoke, it was clear that he loved being on the stage and talking to us. You could almost feel his excitement grow as he got ready to share with us the next great thing that he had up his sleeves. His passion was contagious and everyone in attendance couldn't help but catch it.

I'm not so sure about trying to emulate Steve's trademark jeans & black shirt look for your next presentation. However, understanding how Steve was able to do what he did so well will point you in the right direction.

Chapter 4

I Hear Your Body Talking...

Chapter 4: I Hear Your Body Talking...

So you've been given the chance to talk to the big people. Or maybe to important customers. Or maybe just to a group of new hires, it doesn't really matter — you can blow any of these opportunities if you aren't aware of what your body is saying.

In fact, in certain circumstances, if you don't really believe what you are talking about, your audience will know it because your body language will be screaming "don't believe me — I don't believe what I'm telling you right now!" In order to avoid getting drowned out by yourself, make sure that you listen to what your body is saying.

We've all heard the expression "Appearances matters". Well guess what, they really do.

Thanks to about 50,000 years of evolution all of us have developed an acute ability to size someone up before they say a single word. Guess what: when you take the stage to start a talk to a group, they have already formed an initial opinion of you.

As you start to talk you will either confirm or refute this impression. So let's talk about what you need to do to make your body talk a powerful part of your communication skills:

- **Stand Up Straight Young Man (or Woman)!** This is the simplest thing to do — stand up straight and adopt a stance that exudes confidence, power, and energy no matter how you are currently feeling. If you look like you are in control, then everyone will believe that you are.

- **No Chicken Dancing!** Our arms and hands are amazing parts of our bodies. However, during a presentation if we are not careful they can put on a show all by themselves and that will end up distracting everyone who is watching us. The right thing to do is to keep them loosely dangling by our sides. Note that although this sounds simple, it is sometimes the hardest thing in the world to do!

- **Turn Off The X-Ray Vision:** Eye contact is an important part of any presentation. It's how you make contact with the audience and it can be a very powerful tool. However, avoiding looking through people in the audience or, even worse, staring down specific audience members. This can cause onlookers to become completely distracted and forget to pay attention to what you have to say.

There's a lot more to understanding what your body is saying. Your goal should be to make sure that your audience is not getting mixed messages from what you say and what your body is saying. If done correctly, your body language can help turn you into a powerful communicator.

Chapter 5

5 Ways To Deliver A Disastrous Presentation

Chapter 5: 5 Ways To Deliver A Disastrous Presentation

So you can find self-help info on how to deliver better presentations just about anywhere on the web (including at my blog www.TheAccidentalCommunicator.com); however, where can you find guidance on how to really deliver a disastrous presentation? Well fear not, that's what we'll cover now...

Monica is one of my friends who is a professional speaker by trade. She is very good at what she does which is to teach retail sales folks in the wireless industry how to sell more.

She appears to be about nine feet tall when you meet her for the first time, has an enormous amount of blond hair, and speaks with a Texas drawl that makes it almost impossible to try to not picture her wearing a cowboy hat. Naturally I went to her to get answers to my questions about how to give a bad presentation.

As you can well imagine, Monica was quite surprised when I asked her what I needed to know in order to give a bad presentation – *"... but why would you EVER want to give a bad presentation. Who do you hate that much that you'd force them to sit through that?..."*

Once I explained that I was trying a bit of reverse psychology here and that if I understood what made up a bad presentation, then I'd know what to avoid she calmed down just a bit. She is from Texas you know so calm is always a relative thing with her.

If you really want to do a poor job of presenting, please consider this to be a checklist provided by Monica. If you'd like to do a good job of presenting, then don't do any of these things!

1. **Don't Rehearse**. What me worry? Why bother to practice – you know this stuff inside and out, you'll just go up there and wing it and the crowd will love you because it will seem more natural and less rehearsed than all the other presenters. Yeah right. Look: actors and musicians practice, practice, practice in order to get good enough to perform. What makes you think that you can get away without rehearsing? No matter how silly you look while practicing, you'll look much better when you go to do the real thing!

2. **Don't Tell The Audience Why They Are Sitting In Uncomfortable Chairs**. When you take the stage, you have everyone's attention. When you open your mouth to speak, you will start to lose them. Since you'd really like to keep as much of their attention as possible, you really should explain why you're there. Don't launch into your detailed presentation on how to optimize an Oracle 11g database using only a ball-point pen and a roll of aluminum foil until you connect with the audience by explaining why you've come to tell them this information.

3. **Tell Them What You're Going To Tell Them, Tell Them, And Then Tell Them What You Told Them**. I'm not sure if this was ever a good idea; however, it has become a cornerstone of public speaking courses and books. Too bad it's really bad advice. We live in an age of text messages, iPhones, and TIVO time shifters. Nobody has the time or the energy to sit through a presentation where the content is just being summarized and represented three times over. You always want to lead up to your closing – end with a bang not a whimper. If you are summarizing for your audience, then you'll lose them. Instead tell them that the murder was done by Colonel Mustard in the library with the candlestick.

4. **Use As Many Slides As Possible**. No matter how you feel about PowerPoint you have to admit one thing: it's made creating slides very easy to do. As with most things about PowerPoint, this can be a bad thing. Look, your presentation is all about you and what you have to say, it's not about the slides. Every new slide that you show to your audience will cause them to take their attention away from you to look at the slide. You will then have to fight them to get their attention back. Slides should complement and enhance what you are saying. Try this: use one slide for every 5 minutes of your presentation.

5. **Use Your Slide Deck As A Speech Outline**. We've all seen this done: the presenter turns either 90 or 180 degrees from the audience and stares at the slides on the wall during the entire presentation. The audience spends it's time thinking that they could just read the slides and not have to sit through this entire presentation since the presenter is just reading them to the audience. In a nutshell, this just shows that you didn't take any time to prepare.

Monica told me that she could go on and on (and I believed her), but that these were the top 5 tips that she would provide to anyone who really wanted to do a bad job delivering a presentation. I'm not sure if she's ever going to talk to me again, but at least I got the info that I had asked for.

Chapter 6

Top 9 Bad Habits Of Technical Presenters

Chapter 6: Top 9 Bad Habits Of Technical Presenters

Perhaps you were looking for a top 10 list? I've spent some time thinking about all of the technical presentations that I've given in the past and I was only able to come up with a list of nine really, really bad things that I've done over and over again. Let's take a look at the bad habits that technical presenters make and, as a bonus, we'll see if we can find ways to stop doing them!

1. **Technical Presenter Bad Habit #1: Reading Your Speech.**
   I don't care how technical the material that you are talking about is, you need to connect with your audience during your presentation and you won't be able to do this if you are tied to your notes, your slides, or even a script. Instead, practice, practice, practice. Once you really know your material, then you'll be able to deliver it without notes. Steve Jobs over at Apple did this and that's why he was so good!

2. **Technical Presenter Bad Habit #2: Poor Eye Contact.**
   They say that the eyes are the windows to the soul. Well, you've got to be looking in those windows in order to be able to determine what is going on inside of your audience's heads. Too many of us will spend an entire presentation looking at something, anything, else besides our audience. You need to consciously make an effort to make eye contact with your audience at least 90% of the time that you are speaking.

3. **Technical Presenter Bad Habit #3: Dressing Badly.**
   As a speaker, you always want to be the best dressed person in the room. While you are speaking, your

clothes will be speaking to the audience also. You want them to be saying that you are both successful and confidant. A good looking speaker gets the respect of the audience even before he/she opens their mouth. If you don't feel confident selecting clothes, then get a friend or a salesperson to help you make the right decisions.

4. **Technical Presenter Bad Habit #4: Bad Body Language**. While you are talking, your body will be having a conversation with your audience at the same time. If your hands are fumbling with a pen, coin, or a ring; or if you are pacing, swaying or otherwise making movements that distract the audience from what you are saying, then you are sabotaging your own presentation. The best way to stop doing this is to practice in front of a mirror or videotape your practice. You just might be surprised at what you see!

5. **Technical Presenter Bad Habit #5: Winging It**. If you feel that you know your material or your audience so well that a rehearsal is not needed, please print out the following words and place them on your desk where you can see them: "YOU'RE WRONG!" The first time that you give a presentation is the worst time that you give it. You just keep getting better each time you run through it. John Chambers, the CEO of Cisco, spends countless hours practicing every part of every presentation. If a big & important guy like him is willing to spend the time, then why wouldn't you?

6. **Technical Presenter Bad Habit #6: Being Too Stiff**. This bad habit is in a fight with bad habit #4. Although you don't want your body parts to flap around and distract from what you are saying, you also don't want to be a statue – this will also distract from what you're saying. If you assume a frozen position, then that will

result in a boring presentation for your audience.

7. **Technical Presenter Bad Habit #7: Shooting Your Audience w/ Bullets**.
I've got great news for you – chances are that your audience can read! This means that if you spend your presentation reading bullets that are listed on a slide that everyone in the audience can read for themselves, then you will have done everyone a disservice. Remember the slides are there to serve the speaker, not the other way around.

8. **Technical Presenter Bad Habit #8: Going On, And On, And On**.
Although you may love to hear yourself speak, studies show that you'll start to lose your audience after about 18 minutes or so. One of the golden rules of presentations is that an audience will never hold it against you if you wrap up early; however, they'll blame you if you take too long. This all gets back to practicing your presentation before you give it – trim it ruthlessly!

9. **Technical Presenter Bad Habit #9: Being Boring**.
Your audience has other things that they could be doing instead of listening to you. You need to do something to grab their attention and make them care about what you are talking about. This means that you need to have a powerful opening that seizes their attention from the get go and a closing that wraps it all up.

Chapter 7

Public Speaking Problem: Too Many Questions (From One Person)!

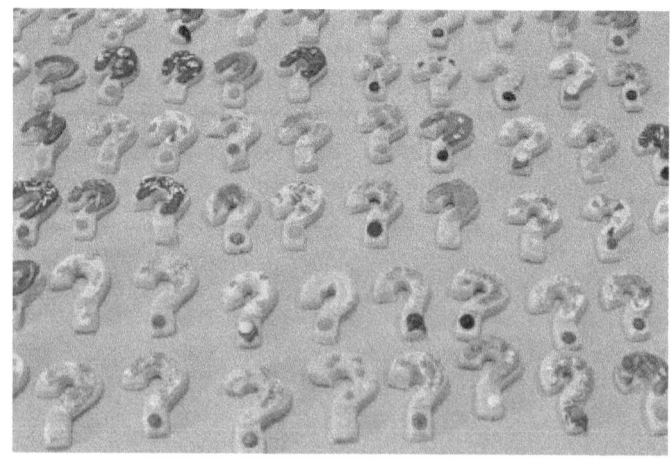

Chapter 7: Public Speaking Problem: Too Many Questions (From One Person)!

As though speaking in public was not difficult enough! Just about every presentation ends up with the obligatory "Question & Answers" opportunity for the audience at the end of the speech.

There are actually three ways your presentation can go at this point in time: (1) nobody asks any questions – sorta embarrassing, but you can live with this as you quickly wrap up and sit down, (2) people ask good questions and you provide good answers – the perfect scenario, (3) some jerk starts asking a whole bunch of questions and just won't give up. Let's spend some time discussing what to do about this last scenario.

The eternal questioner (EC) is one of the strange creatures that lives in the land of public speaking. A close relative to the heckler, the EC is in love with themselves – especially the sound of their own voice.

Experience has shown that the EC is most likely to be found attending your more informal speaking events: team meetings, brainstorming sessions, etc. He/she will generally avoid the big presentations to Senior Management because there is a good chance someone would shoot him/her down at those meetings.

Why does the EC do this? There are many reasons, but the best ones that I can come up with are as follows. The first is that the EC has a story that they want to tell. It really doesn't matter what your presentation is about, they are going to use your Q&A time to tell their story.

The other reason is that they have a whole series of ideas that are just jumping around in their head and they want to spill them out for everyone to see. It really doesn't matter what their motivation is, you're left with a problem on your hands.

How can you deal with an EC? When you encounter an EC the worst thing that you can do is nothing. Your audience is quickly seeing your presentation go from great to bad and if you don't step in, then you'll have to live with their final analysis forever. Here are four steps that you can take to deal with an EC:

1. **Lose the Anger:** You need to realize that the EC is not doing this because you are you. Instead, you've got to realize that the EC does this to everyone – it's not personal. What this means is that the worst thing that you can do is to get angry. Don't – realize that it's just a distraction and lose the anger.

2. **Play To Your Audience:** When the EC reaches a stopping point (or takes a breath!), you need to say something that will show your audience that that you are willing to treat everyone with respect. A phrase such as "Good point, let's talk about it after words." would work. Note that this probably won't shut the EC up, but it will win you points with the rest of the audience.

3. **Realize That Everybody's Got 'Em:** Once again, it's not personal. Some of the greatest communicators of our time such as Jack Welsh, Suzie, Orman, Steve Jobs, etc. have had to deal with ECs. You are not alone!

4. **Make Sure That You Have A Wingman:** In order to head events like this off at the pass, it's always a good idea to coordinate with whoever is running the meeting and have them agree to help you out if you encounter an EC. Let them play the "heavy" once the EC starts to hit his/her stride. Have the organizer step in and tell the EC to sit down and give other audience members a chance

to ask their questions. This way you still have the respect and admiration of the audience.

Chapter 8

Stand Up Straight Young Man! (Public Speaking Tip)

Chapter 8: Stand Up Straight Young Man! (Public Speaking Tip)

So when was the last time that you spent any time thinking about how you breathe? I'm going to guess that it was sometime when you couldn't get air – underwater, someone sitting on your chest, bag over your head, etc.

Since you are reading these words, I'm going to guess that somehow you were able to get that next precious gasp of air and that you've probably not paid any attention to the whole breathing thing since then. However, maybe it's time that you did…

We've all been in the audience when someone gives a speech for the first time. Generally, it doesn't go very well.

One big reason for the disappointing result is that they are generally quite nervous and end up talking VERY fast as they race to get it over and to be allowed to sit down again. As you can probably guess, this is exactly the wrong way to deliver a speech and their breathing has a lot to do with it.

So what's really going on here? Speakers don't show up thinking "Hmm, I bet that if I talk really, really fast things will go well for me." Instead, they are victims of their own bodies.

It all starts with feeling nervous; this releases chemicals into your system that makes your heart start to beat faster. Your breath then follows suit by becoming shallow and fast.

Because you are nervous, you start to bring oxygen only into the upper part of your lungs. This means that your body starts to react to not having enough oxygen despite your rapid breathing rate! Things start to go downhill after this as far as your muscles, nervous system, brain, and even your voice are concerned.

What's a speaker to do? Being aware that everyone gets nervous when they are called upon to talk in public is the first step. The next is to consciously take control of your breath. If you spend some time thinking about how you are breathing, then you'll be able to counteract the negative effects that poor breathing can cause.

How do I control my breathing? There are six steps that you need to think your way through. Your body is automatically doing the same thing; however, you need to take control and make sure that your body is working the way that YOU want it to work. Here's your proper breathing checklist:

1. Check your posture – stand up straight!

2. Relax! (Head, neck, shoulders)

3. Nose – Yes, Mouth – No. Breath thorough your nose, not your mouth.

4. Breathe deeply – fill your lungs all the way down to the bottom.

5. Exhale all the way – get all of that used air out of there.

6. Observe your breath – is it smooth and even, or short and ragged? Change it if needed.

Chapter 9

Welcome To The Pod: Tips On Podcasting For Public Speakers

Chapter 9: Welcome To The Pod: Tips On Podcasting For Public Speakers

So speaking in front of a real, live audience is a great way to communicate. However, we don't always get to control the world that we live in and so sometimes it's just not possible to have you (the speaker) in the same place as all of the people who need to hear your message (your audience).

What's a speaker to do? Back in the olden days, this would be the time that you'd whip out the cassette recorder, make a master tape, and then through the magic of high-speed dubbing you'd crank out as many copies as you needed and off they'd go in the mail. Thank goodness those days are behind us now.

Here in the 21st Century we've now gone all digital. When we want to record our voices to share with others, we no longer reach for the cassette, now we reach for our laptops and iPods to create podcasts.

As easy as it is these days to capture and publish our spoken words, lately I've been running into a lot of really poorly done podcasts and it's got me scratching my head. I mean, aren't these people listening to what they are creating and, just like me, doesn't it make them shudder?

To make sure that you don't get off the beaten path, here are some tips that will help you create a great communication tool your first time at bat:

- **How Do I Record My Voice In The First Place?** You're going to need two things in order to capture your voice on your laptop: a microphone and some software. You can get wacky about microphones if you are a real audiophile; however, just about any one will do.

It turns out that the sound card built into your laptop actually does most of the work, so the physical microphone just has to be good enough – if you already have one, then use it. If you need a recommendation, the Labtec Verse 524 is a good one to go with and you can't beat the price: ~$10.

- **What Software Should I Use?:** Once you have your speech recorded, you are going to want to do at least a bit of editing on it – chop off the false starts at the beginning or trim off the run on bit at the end. Once again, I'm a big advocate for doing this on the cheap and so I'd recommend downloading and using the very popular free (as in beer), open source software that everyone else seems to be using called Audiocity.

- **How Long Should My Recording Be?:** Ok, so this is where you can get yourself into some serious trouble. The longer you speak, the more damage you can do.

  You have no way of actually "seeing" the audience who will be listening to your podcast, so you need to be as brief as possible and keep to your main points. You want to speak long enough so that your listeners get value from what you are saying; however, you don't want to speak so long that they start to look at their watches wondering if you are ever going to wrap this thing up.

  Remember, they are not sitting in an audience so if you lose them, they'll just click you off. As a general rule of thumb, I'd say that you don't want to talk for longer than 15 minutes on a single podcast.

- **What Should I Not Do?:** This is an easy question to answer – get rid of any "umms" and "ahs" that show up when you are speaking. Since there is no live audience, there is a good chance that if you aren't careful you'll start to fill in the blank spots in your speech with these filler sounds and especially on a podcast, they are quite distracting and really take away from your message.

- **How Should I Change My Speaking Voice?:** Stop – don't! Sometimes your microphone, your laptop, or even Audiocity software will let you change how your recorded voice sounds. I've had women friends who have fooled with these settings so much that their recordings made them sound like James Earl Jones was speaking their parts.

  You are better off speaking using your normal voice. It can be quite a shock when you hear your recorded voice the first time; however, spend some time with it and become comfortable with it – everyone else is!

Chapter 10

4 Things A Public Speaker Needs To Know About WebConferencing

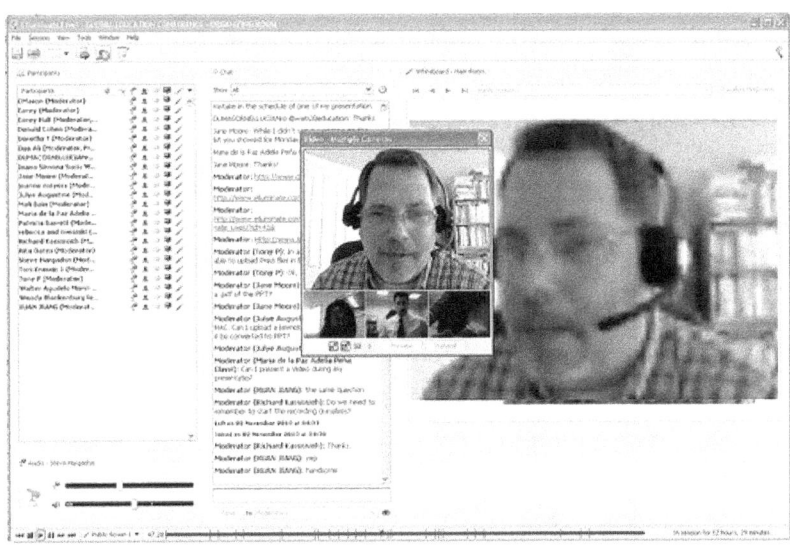

Chapter 10: 4 Things A Public Speaker Needs To Know About WebConferencing

So is delivering a presentation over the web easier or harder than delivering it to a live audience? Just to make sure that we're all on the same page, let's agree on what web conferencing is (hint: it's not sending your PowerPoint presentation to someone via email).

For our purposes, we can define web conferencing as a way to give a presentation, hold an important meeting, or even train employees without requiring the people participating to have to travel. Thanks to phone bridges, PowerPoint decks, and high-speed Internet connections this is now a viable way to deliver presentations.

The technology is pretty slick – you can quickly come up to speed on how to technically DO a web conference. The real trick is to find out how to do a GOOD JOB of presenting using this new technology. Dave Zielinski recently had a chance to talk with Laura Vizzusi and David Goad who work for Cisco's WebEx division. WebEx rules this space on the web so these guys really know what they are talking about. Here are their top four suggestions for web conferencing public speaker wanna be's:

1. **Prep, Prep, Prep:** Just because the medium has changed, does not mean that the rules have changed. Even through you don't have to travel to give the presentation and since, possibly, the audience won't be able to actually see you, some people will be tempted to slack off. DON'T DO IT! You can still put your audience to sleep if you don't deliver a polished presentation.

2. **It's All In The Voice:** How you sound is even more important in a web conference than it is when you are

presenting in person. Whatever you do – don't use a speakerphone! You will sound far away and your voice will fade in and out as you move your head. DO use a headset mic if you can. In fact, stand up and present if at all possible – this will allow you to project your voice better and will allow you to use the full range of your voice.

3. **That's Why They Call Them Visual Aids:** Since your audience won't be able to look at you, they will be spending more time looking at your slides. Make sure they are worth looking at! You are also going to have to keep your slides moving right along in order to keep your audience's attention. Slide transitions and the liberal use of photographs are always good ideas.

4. **Welcome To The 21st Century:** Most web conferencing tools come with a variety of bells and whistles that allow you to interact with your audience during your presentation. Used poorly, you'll tick everyone off. Used correctly, this is a great way to dynamically engage everyone in what you are saying. Tools like interactive polls and on-screen annotations can capture and hold everyone's attention.

Don't forget one of the biggest benefits of web conferencing is that it is very easy to record your presentation. This is a great way to give a presentation once and then use it over and over again...

Chapter 11

Presentation From A Book: How To Do Dramatic Readings

Chapter 11: Presentation From A Book: How To Do Dramatic Readings

In the bag of skills that a public speaker needs to have, there is one that is not used very often: dramatic readings. Now just because we don't use it very often, does not mean that we shouldn't be using it more.

Remember that anything that we can do to make our presentations stand out from everything else that our audience gets assaulted with each and every day will help to make it more memorable (in a good way) and improves the chances of our message "sticking" with our audience. The big questions are when should I use a dramatic reading as a part of my presentation and just how do I go about doing it?

The first question is actually the easiest to answer. A dramatic reading from a book is a great way to do two things: add color to a presentation and add credibility to WHAT you are talking about.

Published authors often have taken a great deal of time to get their words just right. Opening a book during your presentation and reading their words to your audience allows you to capture the time and effort that they put into creating their ideas and enrich your speech by doing so.

Additionally, in order to motivate your audience to make a change or to take some action (the purpose of any presentation), you need to convince them that you know what you are talking about. By reading a passage from a published book perhaps written by a well-known figure in the field that you are talking about, you can reinforce your words by having them appear to support your position.

Now the big question is how best to do a dramatic reading. The problem here is that most of us have very little experience with either listening to or actually doing dramatic readings from a book.

That's why we can turn to Mark McLaughlin who is an author of horror books. Mark is often called on to give speeches that contain, what else?, dramatic readings. He probably does this much more than the rest of us ever will; however, this also means that he can teach us a lot about how to do them correctly.

Here are Mark's top 10 tips for how we can all do dramatic readings as a part of our presentations correctly:

1. **Don't Read From The Book:** Books are great for sitting by a fire and reading. They are quite poor to read from during a presentation: their print is too small, it can be hard to find your place, and turning the page is awkward at best. Instead, copy the pages and blow them up.

2. **Use Voices:** Something that you may not realize is that we all make different characters sound different in our head when we read a book. When you are reading from a book, you need to use a different voice for each character so that your audience doesn't get confused about who is talking or thinking.

3. **Prepare Using A Rainbow:** Mark up what you are going to be reading using many different colored highlighters. This way you will automatically remember to switch voices when you are reading.

4. **Characters Are More Than Just Voices:** Different characters can have different mannerisms and these can be useful when you are reading their lines. Smokers

should have a raspy voice, nervous characters should speak quickly, etc.

5. **Try Out Different Voices:** You won't get it right the first time so be sure to experiment with different voices in order to find the one that will capture the character the best for your audience.

6. **Practice, Practice, Practice:** This is always a good idea and it's even more critical when doing a dramatic reading. McLaughlin recommends that you practice at least a dozen times and even more if you feel that you need it.

7. **The Power Of A Friendship:** Nothing beats live feedback. Try your presentation out on **friends** and see what kind of feedback they give you. This can be worth its weight in gold.

8. **Look At Your Audience While Reading To Them:** You can't do this all the time of course; however, eye contact is always a good idea.

9. **Have A Panic Button Ready:** Look, anyone can lose their place while doing a reading – it happens to all of us. If this happens to you, have a question about the reading ready to ask an audience member. Use the time that they are speaking to find your spot again, mark it with a finger, thank the audience member for their answer and then continue on.

10. **Enjoy Yourself!:** Dramatic readings are done all to rarely in presentations today. The fact that you have been willing to step up, practice, and then deliver a dramatic reading shows that you are better than the average speaker. When your audience sees that you are

enjoying yourself, then they will get into it also and your presentation will be your best ever!

Chapter 12

10 Tips For Little Presentations (Or Presentations To Little People)

Chapter 12: 10 Tips For Little Presentations (Or Presentations To Little People)

So I'm not so sure that that title is clear, but basically what I'm talking about is delivering presentations to young people. I'm talking about elementary school age folks. Like 5-11 years old. Maybe the toughest crowd that you'll ever have to face!

I come up against this tough customer at least once a year when the schools in my area have a "career day" where parents are invited to come and talk to the kids about their careers. The goal is to provide the kids with motivation to study hard and stay in school.

I love my job; however, it's a hard sell to kids who have just been dazzled by the policeman / fireman / soldier who all have cool uniforms and neat utility belts. On top of this career appeal challenge, there's that issue with trying to find the right way to talk to these kids – you know, they really are not young adults just yet…

When I need help in trying to figure out how best to deal with a tough crowd like this, I know that it's best to go talk with an expert. In this case the expert is Caren Neile who is the director of Florida Atlantic University's Storytelling Project. Here are 10 tips for how you can not only survive a presentation to the very young, but also do a good job of it:

1. **Watch Your Height:** Kids are very sensitive to having to look up at a speaker. You need to do everything that you can to "be on their level". One way to do this is to sit on the floor. Another is to sit on a chair – pretty much the opposite of what we tell you to do when speaking to adults!

2. **Don't Start Your Presentation Cold**: One of the key things that you want to happen when you talk with kids is to have them behave and pay attention. This can be hard to do if they don't know you. By spending some time with them **before** you start your presentation you can knock down some of the walls that exist between you and them. By doing this, you can come across as a person that they know and they'll do a better job of paying attention to what you have to say.

3. **Be Real Man**: Kids hate vague "management speak". Remember that their world is pretty much what they see on a daily basis and only the things that they can touch are real. If you speak in big broad terms ("the whole world", "boosting productivity", "over $1B dollars", etc.) they simply won't be able to grasp what you are talking about. Instead, use concrete expressions that they can easily understand ("lots of people", "able to make even more widgets", "enough money to fill this room from floor to ceiling", etc.)

4. **See What I'm Saying**: Props are your friend when you are talking to a young audience. We've raised them to be multi-tasking demons and they'll show you just how good they are at this by tuning you out and working on other tasks while you are talking unless you find a way to keep grabbing their attention. Props are one of the best ways to do this.

5. **Take A Time Out**: How long can you sit and effectively listen to someone? Kids can't pay attention for even that long! Given 'em a break before, during, and after your presentation. They will be forever grateful.

6. **Have Everyone Play A Role**: Much more than adults, kids love to participate in a presentation. They will be itching to do this even if you don't want them to do so.

Caren suggests that you work specific places in your presentation for them to help you out. This will help to keep their interest and will make your presentation even more memorable.

7. **Get Up And Move!:** Once again, we generally like it when adults sit through our presentations. With kids, things are different. If you can find a way to get them to get up and move around as part of your presentation, then they will connect with you and your message better.

8. **Chill Out Man:** With adults, we would often like it if they stood up and started shouting during our presentation – it would show that they were really engaged. With kids, they might just stand up and start shouting because they like to shout. Make sure that you don't get them too riled up during your presentation or things could get out of hand.

9. **Allow Learning To Happen:** We all learn in our own way and kids are no exception to this rule. Some kids will appear to tune you out, may be drawing while you speak, may even get up and walk around. Don't be offended and don't worry about it. This may be how they learn best and you should just let it happen.

It's from the forge of failure that the steel of success is formed.

Hard Work Does Not Guarantee Success, But Success Does Not Happen Without Hard Work.

- Dr. Jim Anderson

Create Speeches That Motivate Your Audiences And Get Your Message Heard!

Dr. Jim Anderson is available to provide training and coaching on the topics that are the most important to people who have to speak in public: how can I create a speech that people want to hear and how can I deliver in a way that will allow me to connect with my audience and get my point across to them?

Dr. Anderson believes that in order to both learn and remember what he says, speakers need to laugh. Each one of his speeches is full of fun and humor so that what he says "sticks" with everyone.

Dr. Anderson's Public Speaking Training Includes:

1. How to plan your next speech: pick your purpose and understand your audience.
2. What's the best way to get PowerPoint and Keynote to work with you, not against you?
3. What do you need to do when you are presenting in order to truly connect with your audience?

Dr. Jim Anderson presents over 100 speeches per year. To invite Dr. Anderson to speak at your event, contact him at: **Phone: 813-418-6970** or **Email:** jim@BlueElephantConsulting.com

Photo Credits:

Cover - By: Shane Kelly (ballinascreen.com)
http://www.flickr.com/photos/29106784@N02/

Chapter 1 - By: UNIONDOCS
http://www.flickr.com/photos/uniondocs/

Chapter 2 - By: Oracle PR
http://www.flickr.com/photos/oracle_images/

Chapter 3 - By: Ben Stanfield
http://www.flickr.com/photos/acaben/

Chapter 4 - By: James McDowell
http://www.flickr.com/photos/jaromcdowell/

Chapter 5 - By: Rupert Colley
http://www.flickr.com/photos/historyinanhour/

Chapter 6 - By: Washington DNR
http://www.flickr.com/photos/wastatednr/

Chapter 7 - By: Scott McLeod
http://www.flickr.com/photos/mcleod/

Chapter 8 - By: John
http://www.flickr.com/photos/mtsofan/

Chapter 9 - By: José Maria Silveira Neto
http://www.flickr.com/photos/silveiraneto/

Chapter 10 - By: Hazel Owen
http://www.flickr.com/photos/24289877@N02/

Chapter 11 - By: Roland Legrand
http://www.flickr.com/photos/rolandlegrand/

Chapter 12 - By: waterdotorg
http://www.flickr.com/photos/waterdotorg/

Other Books By The Author

Product Management

- Product Development Lessons For Product Managers: How Product Managers Can Create Successful Products

- Customer Lessons For Product Managers: Techniques For Product Managers To Better Understand What Their Customers Really Want

- Product Failure Lessons For Product Managers: Examples Of Products That Have Failed For Product Managers To Learn From

- Communication Skills For Product Managers: The Communication Skills That Product Managers Need To Know How To Use In Order To Have A Successful Product

- How To Have A Successful Product Manager Career: The Things That You Need To Be Doing TODAY In Order To Have A Successful Product Manager Career

- Product Manager Product Success: How to keep your product on track and make it become a success

Public Speaking

- How To Rehearse In Order To Give The Perfect Speech: How to effectively rehearse your next speech to that your message be remembered forever!

- Secrets To Creating The Perfect Speech: How to create a speech that will make your message be remembered forever!

- Secrets To Organizing The Perfect Speech: How to organize the best speech of your life!

- Secrets To Planning The Perfect Speech

CIO Skills

- How CIOs Can Make Innovation Happen: Tips And Techniques For CIOs To Use In Order To Make Innovation Happen In Their IT Department

- CIO Communication Skills Secrets: Tips And Techniques For CIOs To Use In Order To Become Better Communicators

- Managing Your CIO Career: Steps That CIOs Have To Take In Order To Have A Long And Successful Career

- CIO Business Skills: How CIOs can work effectively with the rest of the company!

IT Manager Skills

- Secrets Of Effective Leadership For IT Managers: Tips And Techniques That IT Managers Can Use In Order To Develop Leadership Skills

- IT Manager Career Secrets: Tips And Techniques That IT Managers Can Use In Order To Have A Successful Career

- IT Manager Budgeting Skills: How IT Managers Can Request, Manage, Use, And Track Their Funding

Negotiating

- Learn How To Argue In Your Next Negotiation: How To Develop The Skill Of Effective Arguing In A Negotiation In Order To Get The Best Possible Outcome

- How To Open Your Next Negotiation: How To Start A Negotiation In Order To Get The Best Possible Outcome

- Preparing For Your Next Negotiation: What You Need To Do BEFORE A Negotiation Starts In Order To Get The Best Possible Deal

Miscellaneous

- Power Distribution Unit (PDU) Secrets: What Everyone Who Works In A Data Center Needs To Know!

- Making The Jump: How To Land Your Dream Job When You Get Out Of College!

"Presentation techniques that will transform a speech into a memorable event"

This book has been written with one goal in mind – to show you how you can present a powerful and effective speech We're going to show you how to use the tools that every speaker has to deliver a great speech!

Let's Make Your Next Speech A Success!

What You'll Find Inside:

- **I WANT TO PRESENT JUST LIKE STEVE JOBS**

- **TOP 9 BAD HABITS OF TECHNICAL PRESENTERS**

- **PUBLIC SPEAKING PROBLEM: TOO MANY QUESTIONS (FROM ONE PERSON)!**

- **4 THINGS A PUBLIC SPEAKER NEEDS TO KNOW ABOUT WEBCONFERENCING**

Dr. Jim Anderson brings his 25 years of real-world experience to this book. He's delivered speeches at some of the world's largest firms as well as at many conferences. He's going to show you what you need to do in order to make your next speech a success!

www.ingramcontent.com/pod-product-compliance
Lightning Source LLC
Chambersburg PA
CBHW071811170526
45167CB00003B/1264